CELTIC AND MEDIEVAL
DESIGNS

CELTIC AND MEDIEVAL
DESIGNS
A COLLECTION OF INSPIRATIONAL PROJECTS

DOROTHY WOOD

Photographs by Lucy Mason

HERMES
HOUSE

This edition published in the UK in 1997 by Hermes House

This edition published in Canada by Book Express,
a division of Raincoast Books, 8680 Cambie Street,
Vancouver, British Columbia V6P 6M9

Hermes House is an imprint of
Anness Publishing Limited
Hermes House
88-89 Blackfriars Road
London SE1 8HA

ISBN 1-901289-96-6

Publisher: Joanna Lorenz
Project Editor: Joanne Rippin
Designer: Janet James
Photographer: Lucy Mason
Charts: Ethan Danielson

This book has previously been published as part of a larger compendium,
The Ultimate Cross Stitch Companion

Printed and bound in Hong Kong

1 3 5 7 9 10 8 6 4 2

CONTENTS

THREADS

Although stranded cotton is probably the most popular and versatile thread for cross stitch embroidery, there is an amazing range of different threads available.

Coton perlé produces attractive raised stitches and tapestry wool makes big, chunky cross stitches on a seven or eight count canvas. Some of the projects in this book use other familiar threads such as coton à broder or soft cotton but many are worked in new threads such as silky Marlitt or the more rustic flower thread which is ideal for stitching on linen. New threads are appearing on the market all the time. Look out for unusual flower threads which have been dyed in shaded natural colours and metallic threads which have been specially made for cross stitching.

TAPESTRY WOOL

Although traditionally associated with needlepoint, tapestry wool is also suitable for some cross stitch. It is usually worked on a chunky seven count canvas and makes a warm, hard-wearing cover for cushions, stools and chairs.

FLOWER THREAD OR NORDIN

This rustic cotton thread is ideal for working on evenweave linen fabrics. In thickness it is equivalent to two or three strands of stranded cotton. It is available in solid colours, but look out for the space-dyed skeins.

MARLITT

A lustrous rayon thread, Marlitt has been introduced to provide the sheen and beauty of silk at an economical price. Although only available in solid colours, it has four strands, allowing the colours to be mixed "in the needle".

COTON PERLÉ

This twisted thread has a distinct pearly sheen and is available in over 300 different colours. It comes in several different thicknesses and is generally used to produce a slightly raised effect on a variety of fabrics.

STRANDED COTTON

This is the most popular embroidery thread and is available in over 400 different colours. It is a versatile thread which can be divided into six separate strands. The separated strands of several colours can be intermingled to create a mottled effect when stitched.

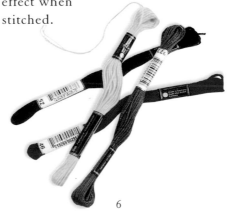

METALLIC THREADS

Although traditionally unsuitable for cross stitch embroidery, some metallic threads are now specially made to sew through fabric. They are available in a range of colours as well as gold and silver. Finer metallic threads known as blending filaments can be worked together with strands of embroidery thread to add an attractive sparkle or sheen.

FABRICS

Evenweave fabrics have the same number of threads running in each direction. The number of threads in each 2½ cm (1 in) of fabric determines the gauge or "count". The larger the number of threads, the finer the fabric. Aida and Hardanger are woven and measured in blocks of threads. However, cross stitches worked on 28 count linen are the same size as those on 14 count Aida because the stitches are worked over two threads of linen.

LINEN

Traditionally pure linen was used, but there are now several different mixed fibre evenweave fabrics in a wide range of colours.

AIDA AND HARDANGER

These popular fabrics have groups of threads woven together to produce distinctive blocks over which the embroidery is worked.

Aida comes in 8–18 count whereas Hardanger is a 22 count fabric. It can be used for fine stitching or worked as an 11 count fabric.

EVENWEAVE BANDS

Aida or evenweave bands come in a variety of widths. Some are plain and others have decorative edges. Once stitched, these bands can be applied to a background fabric or made up into bows, tie-backs or bags.

FANCY WEAVES

Fabrics specially woven with distinct areas for cross stitching are suitable for making into napkins, tablecloths and cot covers. There are also some unusual evenweaves which have linen or Lurex threads interwoven into the fabric for special effects.

CANVAS

Double and single thread canvas is usually associated with needlepoint but can be used successfully for cross stitch embroidery. Wool and coton perlé are particularly suitable threads for using when stitching on canvas.

WASTE CANVAS

A non-interlocked canvas is used to work cross stitch on non-evenweave fabric or ready-made items. It is specially made so that it can be frayed and removed after the cross stitch is worked.

NON-FRAY FABRICS

Plastic canvas, vinyl weave and stitching paper are all used for cross stitch projects where it is important that the fabric should not fray.

ADDITIONAL FABRICS

Iron-on interfacing is sometimes used to provide a backing for the cross stitch design.

Fusible bonding web is generally used for appliqué.

1: linens; 2: plastic canvas, stitching paper, fusible bonding web, iron-on interfacing; 3: aida and linen bands; 4: 14 and 10 count waste canvas; 5: aida and white Hardanger; 6: canvases; 7: fancy weaves.

TECHNIQUES:BEGINNING

PREPARING THE FABRIC

Many of the projects in this book use evenweave fabrics which tend to fray easily, therefore it is advisable to finish the edges before starting the embroidery. An allowance has been made for neatening the edges in calculating the materials needed.

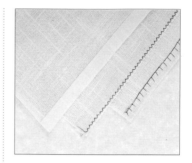

MASKING TAPE

A quick method for projects worked on interlocking bar frames. The tape can be stapled or pinned to a frame.

ZIGZAG

Machine-stitched zigzag is used when embroidering parts of a garment since the seams will be neatened ready to stitch together.

BLANKET STITCH

This is the best all round method of neatening evenweave fabric. Either turn a small hem or stitch round the raw edge.

LEFT TO RIGHT: masking tape, zigzag and blanket stitch.

COVERING A HOOP

Embroidery hoops (frames) have two rings, one is solid and the other has a screw-fastening. The fabric is sandwiched between the two rings and the screw-fastening adjusted to keep the fabric taut. In order to protect the fabric and stitches from damage, the inner ring is wrapped with narrow cotton tape. Remember that some delicate fabrics can be damaged in an embroidery hoop (frame). In these cases it is advisable to use a large hoop which extends beyond the cross stitch area. Interlocking bar frames are ideal for small projects and a rotating frame is best for large pieces of work.

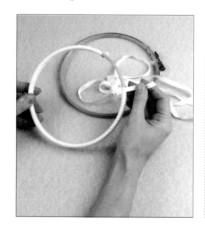

STARTING & FINISHING THREADS

There are several ways to begin a piece of cross stitch. Finish by sliding the needle under several stitches and trimming the end.

1 Fold a length of cotton in half and thread into the needle. Work the first half of the cross stitch, then thread the needle through the loop on the reverse side.

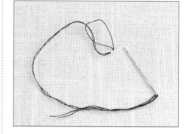

2 Leave a length of 5 cm (2 in) thread at the back of the fabric and weave this in when you have worked a block of stitches.

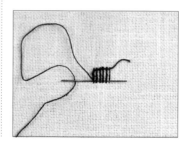

WASTE CANVAS

This technique allows charted cross stitch to be worked on non-evenweave fabric or ready-made items such as towels and cushions. Waste canvas is specially made so that the threads can be easily removed. It is only available in 10 and 14 count but you could use ordinary canvas provided that the threads are not interlocked.

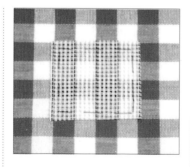

1 Tack (baste) a piece of canvas onto the area to be stitched. Make sure there will be plenty of canvas round the design once it is complete.

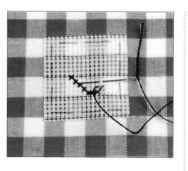

2 Work the cross stitch design over the canvas and through the fabric. Take care to make all the stitches as even as you possibly can.

3 Once complete, fray the canvas and pull the threads out one at a time. It will be easier if you tug the canvas gently to loosen the threads.

TECHNIQUES:FINISHING

MITRED CORNER

Tablecloths and mats can be finished neatly with mitred corners. These reduce bulk and make a secure hem which can be laundered safely.

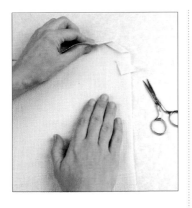
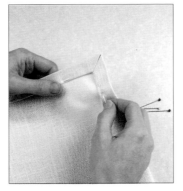

1 Fold the hem, run your fingers along and open out. Cut across the corner from crease to crease and refold the hem.

2 Turn under a further 0.5 cm (1/4 in) and pin the hem in place. Slip stitch the mitred corner and machine or hand stitch the hem.

STRETCHING

As a general rule embroidery should always be stretched using thread so that it can be easily removed and cleaned in the future. However, small projects which may be kept for only a limited time can be quickly and successfully mounted using double-sided tape.

1 Cut the card (cardboard) to the required size and stick double-sided tape along all the edges. Trim across the corners and remove the paper backing. Stretch the fabric onto the tape and mitre the corners neatly.

MOUNTING

If a project such as a sampler or picture is likely to be kept for a long time, great care should be taken in mounting the finished work. Acid-free mount board (backing board) or paper should be used under the embroidery and glue or tape which leave an acid residue on the fabric should be avoided.

The following easy method of mounting ensures that the embroidery will be absolutely straight and exactly where you want it.

1 Cut the mount board to size and mark the mid point across the top and bottom of the board. Allow for a wider border at the bottom if required. Mark the mid point of the embroidery at each side of the board and draw in the lines. Lay the embroidery face down on a flat surface and place the mount board on top of it.

2 Line up the guidelines on the embroidery with the lines on the board. Fold the top edge over and put a pin into the mount board at the centre line. Stretch the fabric slightly and put another pin at the bottom. Repeat the process at the sides. Work your way along each edge from the centre out putting in pins every 2.5 cm (1 in) keeping the grain of the fabric straight.

3 Using a long length of double thread, sew from side to side spacing the stitches about 12 mm (1/2 in) apart. Join in more thread using an overhand knot. Once complete lift the threads up one at a time to pull them tight and secure. Mitre or fold the corners and repeat along the remaining sides.

ADDITIONS

Most embroidery is embellished by the addition of trimmings, and cross stitch is no exception. Whether it is an Asian design with shisha mirrors and tassels or a traditional English lavender bag edged with Victorian lace, the "additions" always enhance the cross stitch design and add the finishing touch to an attractive piece.

BEADS

Beads are attached using a double thread and in contrast to all other forms of embroidery, begun with a securely tied knot. Sew the beads on individually, as if you were stitching the first half of a cross stitch.

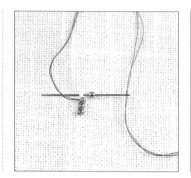

BUTTONS

Buttons with four holes can be stitched on with a large cross stitch to make a very attractive addition to a design.

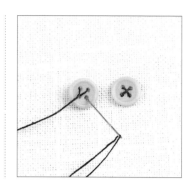

RIBBON

Ribbon looks very effective when used to create a grid for a repeat design of small cross stitch motifs. The ribbon is laid straight along the grain before the cross stitch has been worked. Choose a ribbon which is the same width as one cross stitch. If the ribbon is to be applied diagonally it is easier to work the cross stitch motifs first.

1 Pin the strips of ribbon in position in one direction and pin the rest across the top. Check that the spacing is correct, then tack the ends.

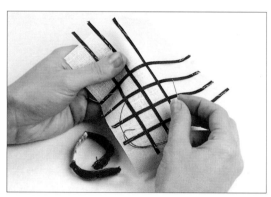

2 Sew a cross stitch at each junction where the ribbons overlap. Remember that if the ribbons are applied diagonally, the cross stitch will be upright.

MAKING A CORD

Embroidery threads are ideal for making into fine cord. The threads can be all one colour or mixed colours to match each particular project.

The amount of thread you need depends on the final thickness of the cord required. As a rough guide, a 1 m (39 in) length of threads ready to twist will make a cord about 40 cm (16 in) long.

1 Cut several lengths of thread, two and a half times the final cord length. Fix one end to a secure point. Slip a pencil through the threads at the other end and twist the pencil like a propeller.

2 Keep turning until the cord begins to twist together. Hold the middle of the cord and bring the ends together. Smooth any kinks with your fingers and tie the ends with an overhand knot.

SHISHA MIRROR

These irregular pieces of mirror are stitched on to garments and hangings as a protection against evil. If spirits see themselves reflected in the mirror then, it is believed, they will flee.

Traditional shisha mirrors can be bought from ethnic suppliers, but large modern sequins are a suitable alternative. As extra security, stick the mirror or sequins in position using a small piece of double-sided tape or a dab of glue.

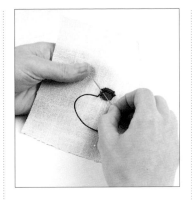

1 Sew two threads across the shisha from top to bottom. Sew across the shisha in the other direction looping the thread round each laid thread to create a framework.

2 Bring the needle up close to the shisha, make a loop through the framework, cross over the loop and pull the thread gently towards you. Take the needle back to the reverse side.

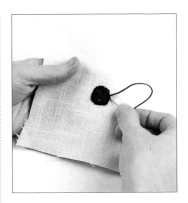

3 Continue round the shisha beginning each stitch between the ends of the previous loop. Finish the thread off on the reverse side.

MAKING TASSELS

One of the prettiest ways to complete a project is to make your own tassels from threads which were used in the embroidery. There are many different ways to make tassels, but most use the same basic technique.

The two following methods are both easy to make. The first tassel is ideal for stitching on to the corners of cushions, mats or bookmarks whereas the second is worked over the end of a cord or rouleau and produces a very professional result. Make the tassels more ornate by adding beads or stitching rows of interlocking blanket stitch round the head until it is completely covered.

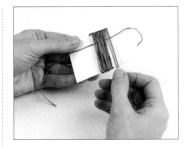

1 Cut a piece of card (cardboard) slightly deeper than the finished length of the tassel. Wind threads round the card as required and slip a length of thread underneath.

2 Cut along the bottom of the threads and tie the bundle together using a sailor's knot. This is like a reef knot, but the thread is twisted round twice before pulling it tight.

3 Wrap another length of thread round the tassel to form a neck and tie off as before. Trim the ends neatly.

1 Wind threads round the card (cardboard) and cut along one side. Tie a knot near the end of the cord or rouleau and place it in the middle of the bundle of threads.

2 Enclose the knot with the threads and tie a separate length of thread around just above the knot.

3 Hold the cord and bring all the threads down together. Wrap a length of cord round underneath the knot and tie off securely as before. Trim the tassel ends neatly.

MEDIEVAL TIEBACKS

*These beautiful chunky tiebacks are the ideal size to hold back
a big heavy curtain for the front door.*

YOU WILL NEED

*70 cm (³⁄₄ yd) natural
hessian fabric*

scissors

pins

tacking (basting) thread

needle

*tapestry wool Anchor two
10 m skeins of 8400, four of
8592 and five of 8630*

tapestry needle

embroidery hoop (frame)

70 cm (³⁄₄ yd) lining fabric

70 cm (³⁄₄ yd) wadding (batting)

sewing thread

two large brass curtain rings

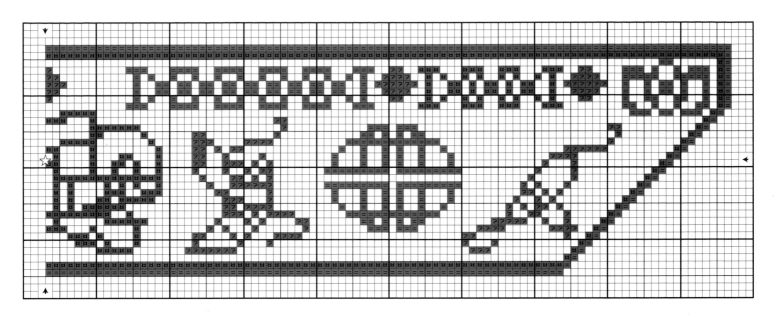

WORKING THE CROSS STITCH

The size of these tiebacks will depend very much on the type of hessian you buy. You can adjust the size to match the curtains. Mark off 20 threads in each direction with pins and measure. This will be equivalent to 10 squares on the chart. Work out the length and depth required and add extra for fringing. Cut a piece of hessian the required size. Tack (baste) guidelines in both directions across the hessian and work the cross stitch over two threads. Once complete, press on the wrong side and trim to 12 mm (½ in).

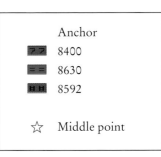

	Anchor
⁊⁊	8400
═ ═	8630
H H	8592
☆	Middle point

1 To make up: cut the lining fabric the same size and fold under a 12 mm (½ in) seam allowance. Cut a piece of wadding (batting) slightly smaller than the pressed lining. Lay the tieback face down and put the wadding on top. Pin the lining through all the layers and hem close to the cross stitch.

2 Sew a curtain ring on the inside at each end of the tieback. Make a fringe by carefully fraying the hessian with a blunt needle as far up as the stitching. Make a second tieback in the same way, if required.

MEDIEVAL CUSHION

Young teenagers will love the bright colours and bold heraldic patterns in this design. The cushion is the ideal size for lounging on a bed.

YOU WILL NEED

46 cm (18 in) square of 7 count Sudan canvas

needle

tacking (basting) thread

tapestry wool Anchor 8004, 8016, 8114, 8140, 8218, 8414, 8588, 8714, 8788, 8784, 9078, 9096, 9768

tapestry needle

rotating frame

pins

scissors

180 cm (2 yd) natural cord piping

sewing thread

sewing machine

46 x 56 cm (18 x 22 in) cream backing fabric

40 cm (16 in) cushion pad

WORKING THE CROSS STITCH

Tack (baste) guidelines across the centre of the canvas in both directions. Work the cross stitch and once it is completed, block to even out the stitches and square up the design.

1 To make up: tack (baste) the piping round the edge of the cross stitch and machine in place. Stitch a 1 cm (³⁄₈ in) hem on both short ends of the backing fabric. Cut crossways down the centre and overlap the hems to make a 30 cm (12 in) square.

2 Tack the backing pieces together and pin on top of the cross stitch with right sides facing. Tack and machine round the sides.

3 Trim the seams and cut across the corners before turning through. Press lightly and insert the cushion pad.

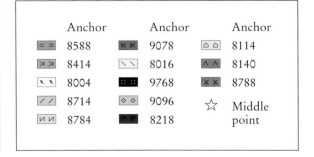

	Anchor		Anchor		Anchor
= =	8588	x x	9078	△ △	8114
⋗ ⋗	8414	\ \	8016	∧ ∧	8140
x x	8004	▓	9768	x x	8788
/ /	8714	◇ ◇	9096	☆	Middle point
И И	8784	▓	8218		

CELTIC CUSHION

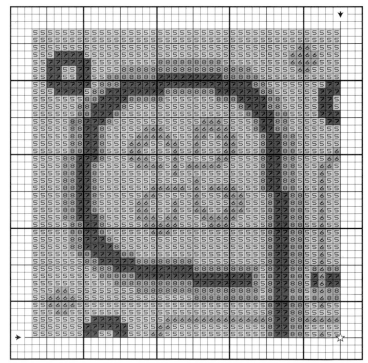

This cushion will look most effective teamed with several others in different shades of blue and yellow and scattered on a couch.

YOU WILL NEED

35 cm (14 in) square of 7 count Sudan canvas

tacking (basting) thread

needle

tapestry wool Anchor 8 skeins of 8704, 4 skeins of 8896, 2 skeins each of 8020 & 8836

tapestry needle

rotating frame

pins

scissors

125 cm (1⅓ yd) blue cord piping

sewing thread

sewing machine

30 x 38 cm (12 x 15 in) deep blue backing fabric

30 cm (12 in) cushion pad

WORKING THE CROSS STITCH

Tack (baste) guidelines across the centre of the canvas in both directions. Work the cross stitch and block once completed to even out the stitches and square up the design.

1 To make up: tack (baste) the piping round the edge of the cross stitch and machine in place. Stitch a 1 cm (⅜ in) hem on both short ends of the backing fabric. Cut crossways down the centre and overlap the hems to make a 30 cm (12 in) square. Tack (baste) the backing pieces together and pin on top of the cross stitch with right sides facing.

2 Tack round all the sides and machine. Trim the seams and cut across the corners before turning through. Press lightly and insert the cushion pad.

	Anchor		Anchor		
5 5	8704	7 7	8836	☆	Middle point
6 6	8020	8 8	8896		

FIREGUARD

Fitted into a fireguard, this fantastic dragon design makes a wonderful screen in front of an empty fire.

tacking (basting) thread

needle

51 x 61 cm (20 x 24 in) grey/blue 28 count Quaker evenweave linen

stranded cotton Anchor two skeins of 1014 and 891

one skein of 273, 274, 357, 403, 779, 830, 831, 849, 853, 855, 856, 868, 875, 877, 898, 900, 943, 945, 5975, 8581

tapestry needle

embroidery hoop (frame)

mount board (backing board)

craft knife

safety ruler

strong thread

fireguard

WORKING THE CROSS STITCH

Although this is a large project, it is sewn on evenweave linen and it can be worked a small area at a time, in a small round embroidery frame to make it easier to handle.

1 Tack (baste) guidelines across middle of the linen in both directions and work the cross stitch over two threads using two strands of cotton. Work the backstitch on the wings using a single strand of 900 and all other backstitch using two strands of 403.

2 To make up: press the embroidery on the reverse side. Cut the mount board (backing board) to fit the fireguard. Stretch the embroidery over the mount board and fit into the fireguard.

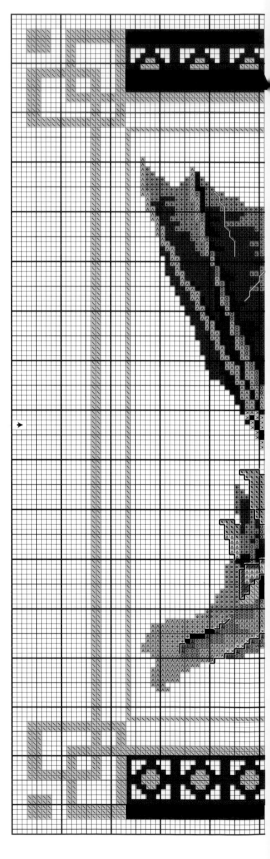

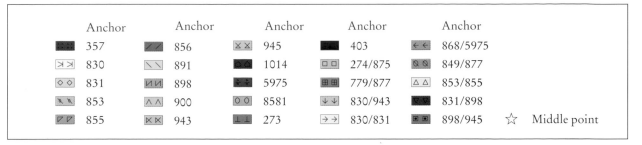

	Anchor		Anchor		Anchor		Anchor		Anchor		
	357		856		945		403		868/5975		
	830		891		1014		274/875		849/877		
	831		898		5975		779/877		853/855		
	853		900		8581		830/943		831/898		
	855		943		273		830/831		898/945	☆	Middle point

NAPKIN RING

These unusual napkin rings will look very elegant slipped around plain linen napkins.

YOU WILL NEED

5 x 15 cm (2 x 6 in)
10 count single canvas
tapestry needle
stranded cotton Anchor 70, 276
scissors
5 x 15 cm (2 x 6 in) cream felt
needle

WORKING THE CROSS STITCH

Work the design using all six strands of cotton. The stitches will lie better if you separate the strands and put them together again before sewing. Press the embroidery on the wrong side once completed.

1 To make up: trim across the corners and fold the excess canvas over to the wrong side.

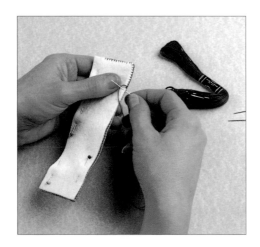

2 Cut the felt to size and sew in place using buttonhole stitch. Bring the ends together and buttonhole stitch through the previous stitching to complete.

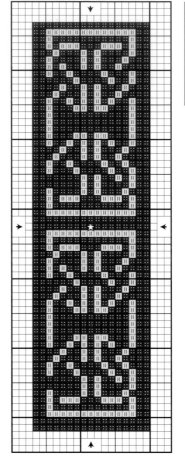

Anchor	
‖ ‖	276
⠿	70
☆	Middle point

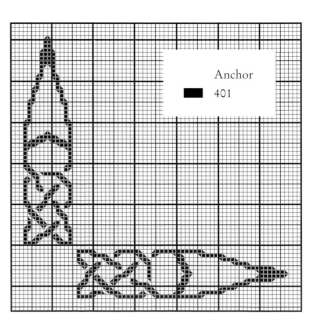

Anchor	
■	401

18

NAPKIN

This Celtic knot design is quick and easy to sew.
Finish the napkins with a simple frayed edge.

WORKING THE CROSS STITCH

Tack (baste) guidelines 5 cm (2 in) in from the edge along two sides of the linen. Work the design in the corner as shown using two strands of cotton over two threads. Press gently on the reverse side when complete.

1. To make up: cut along the grain about 4 cm (1½ in) from the stitching to give a straight edge to the napkin. Withdraw the linen threads to make a 2½ cm (1 in) deep fringe all round.

YOU WILL NEED

40 cm (16 in) square of pale grey 28 count evenweave linen

tacking (basting) thread

needle

tapestry needle

stranded cotton Anchor 401

small embroidery hoop (flexihoop)

scissors

CHAIR COVER

Renovate a worn mahogany chair cover with this warm and comfortable wool cross stitch design. This cover fits a standard-sized dining room chair with a drop-in seat.

YOU WILL NEED

56 cm (22 in) square of 7 count Sudan canvas

tacking (basting) thread

rotating frame

tapestry needle

tapestry wool DMC 5 skeins of 7406, 4 skeins of 7472, 4 skeins of 7544, 7 skeins of 7590, 9 skeins of 7591

scissors

upholsterer's tacks

hammer

56 cm (22 in) square of calico

padded seat frame

WORKING THE CROSS STITCH

Tack (baste) guidelines across the centre of the canvas in both directions. Fit the canvas onto a rotating frame and work the cross stitch, beginning in the centre. Once the cross stitch is complete, block the embroidered panel to even out the stitches and square up the canvas. Press on the reverse side.

1 To make up: beginning in the middle of the front edge, stretch the canvas over the padded seat frame and secure on the underside with a tack. Working out from the centre, hammer tacks in every 5 cm (2 ins). Repeat the process on the rear of the seat and then stretch the sides. Trim away any excess canvas on the corners to reduce the bulk.

2 Tack a square of calico to the underside to finish.

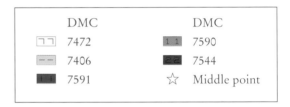

	DMC			DMC
⊓⊓	7472		1 1	7590
– –	7406		2 2	7544
1 1	7591		☆	Middle point

LADY IN THE TOWER

This simple, elegant design was inspired by the rich colours
of a medieval illuminated manuscript.

YOU WILL NEED

25 x 30 cm (10 x 12 in) white
22 count Hardanger

tacking (basting) thread

needle

scissors

stranded cotton DMC 310,
317, 321, 353, 415, 434,
740, 743, 798, 912

tapestry needle

interlocking bar fràme

mount board (backing board)

craft knife

strong thread

picture frame

WORKING THE CROSS STITCH

Tack (baste) guidelines across the centre of the Hardanger in both directions. Beginning in the centre, work the cross stitches over two pairs of threads using three strands of cotton.

1 To make up: once the cross stitch is complete, work the back stitch using three strands of cotton.

2 Remove the tacking (basting) thread. Press on the wrong side. Cut the mount board (backing board) to the required size. Stretch the embroidery and fit it into a frame which complements the design.

	DMC		DMC		Backstitch
= =	353	↗↗	798	—	310
■	321	╱╱	310		
＞＞	740	＼＼	415	☆	Middle point
◇◇	743	＼∖	317		
▨	912	∧∧	434		

ILLUMINATED LETTER

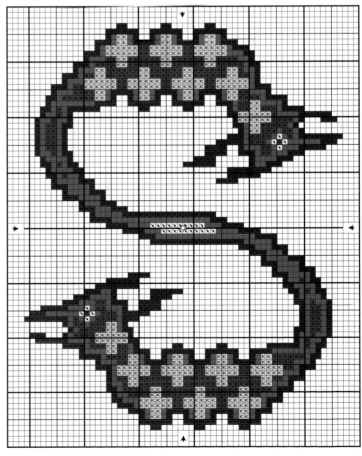

Complete this project with a simple pine frame, painted to match one of the embroidery thread colours.

YOU WILL NEED

*15 cm (6 in) square of cream
28 count evenweave linen*

tacking (basting) thread

needle

*stranded cotton DMC 312,
367, 3046, 3721*

tapestry needle

gold thread DMC Art.284

pine frame

paint, e.g. Colourman 102

paint brush

mount board (backing board)

craft knife

strong thread

WORKING THE CROSS STITCH

Tack (baste) guidelines across the centre of the linen in both directions. Work the cross stitch design over one thread using single strands of cotton and double strands of gold thread.

1 To make up: remove the tacking (basting) thread and press lightly on the wrong side.

2 Paint the frame with two coats of paint to match the embroidery and allow to dry.

3 Cut the mount board (backing board) to size. Lay the mount board on the reverse side of the linen, checking that the design is in the centre. Stretch the embroidery and fit into the frame.

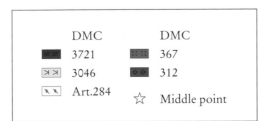

	DMC		DMC
▬	3721	▦	367
⊳	3046	◈	312
⊾	Art.284	☆	Middle point

23

CELTIC BAG

This versatile bag looks attractive, but it is also very practical, and strong enough to carry the vegetables and even a bag of potatoes home.

YOU WILL NEED

scissors

50 cm (½ yd) Antique Aida 27 count Linda, Zweigart E1235

tacking (basting) thread

needle

stranded cotton DMC 335, 400, 772, 783, 800, 890, 931, 938, 988, 3750

tapestry needle

embroidery hoop (frame)

18 cm (7 in) square of lightweight iron-on interfacing

sewing thread

150 cm (½ yd) calico lining

sewing machine

WORKING THE CROSS STITCH

Cut two 41 x 45 cm (16 x 18 in) pieces of linen for the bag. Tack (baste) a guideline lengthways down the centre of one piece. Mark the top edge of the bag by tacking a line crossways 4½ cm (1¾ in) down from the top. Tack a guideline crossways in the centre of the marked panel. Beginning in the centre, work the cross stitches over two threads using two strands of thread. The backstitches are worked in several different colours – body 938, tail 3750 and tongue 355. When the embroidery is complete, press on the wrong side. Ensure the design is square on before ironing the interfacing onto the reverse side. This will help to stabilize the embroidery.

DMC
335
400
772
783
800
890
931
938
988
3750

Backstitch

— 335

— 3750

— 938

☆ Middle point

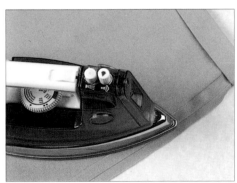

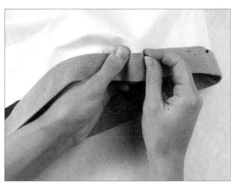

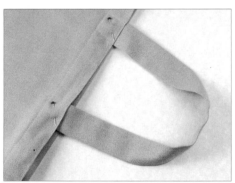

1 To make up: with right sides together, sew down both sides and across the bottom. Trim across the corners and press the seams flat. Make a lining in the same way using two 41 cm (16 in) squares of calico, then stitch again just outside the first row of stitches for extra strength.

2 Fold over 12 mm (½ in) at the top edge of the bag, fold over again along the tacked line and press. Turn the bag through to the right side and insert the calico lining, tucking it under the folded edge. Pin, tack and top stitch along both edges of the hem.

3 Cut two 10 x 45 cm (4 x 18 in) pieces of linen for the straps. Fold them in half lengthways and stitch 12 mm (½ in) from the cut edge, leaving the ends open. Press the seam open and turn through. Press again making sure that that the seam lies down the centre. Zig-zag across the ends. Pin the handles 10 cm (4 in) in from each edge and stitch securely.

COVERED BUTTONS

*Add a touch of elegance to a plain black coat or cardigan
with these sparkly medieval buttons. This design will cover 3 cm
(1¼ in) buttons, but could be adapted for other sizes.*

YOU WILL NEED

*black 27 count Linda,
Zweigart E1235*

tapestry needle

stranded cotton Anchor white

*fine antique gold braid
Kreinik 221*

*small embroidery hoop
(flexihoop)*

scissors

thin card (cardboard)

quilter's pencil

needle

sewing thread

*3 cm (1¼ in)
self-cover buttons*

WORKING THE CROSS STITCH

Work each button design within a 5 cm (2 in) area
and press on the reverse side when completed.

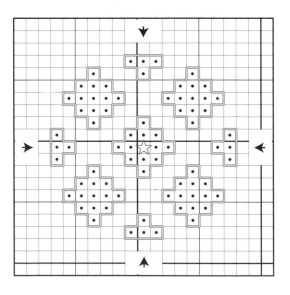

Anchor

·· White

Backstitch

— Kreinik Antique
Gold 221 fine braid

☆ Middle point

1 To make up: cut out a 4 cm (1½ in)
card (cardboard) circle and then cut
out a smaller circle in the centre to make
a card ring. (This lets you see the centre
of the stitches). Position the card ring over
the embroidery and draw round the
outside of it with a pencil.

2 Cut out the button cover and work a
row of tiny running stitches round
the edge. Lay the button on the reverse
side of the cover, pull up the stitches
tightly and secure. Press the back onto the
button to complete.

STOOL COVER

*Add a soft, warm cover to a simple wooden stool or use
the finished design to upholster a footstool.*

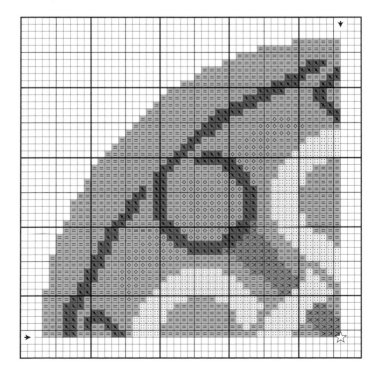

YOU WILL NEED

*40 cm (16 in) square of
7 count Sudan canvas*

rotating frame

tacking (basting) thread

needle

scissors

tapestry needle

*tapestry wool Anchor 6 skeins of
8024, 2 skeins each of 8016,
8106 and 8138, 1 skein of 8136*

*28 cm (11 in) square of thick
wadding (batting)*

double-sided tape

28 cm (11 in) diameter stool

*1 m (1 yd) of 3 cm (1¼ in)
wide dark brown braid*

sewing thread

WORKING THE CROSS STITCH

Tack (baste) guidelines across the
centre of the canvas in both directions
and work the cross stitch in wool.

Once the cross stitch is complete,
block the design to even out the
stitches and trim to 4 cm (1½ in).

1 To make up: cut the
wadding (batting) to
fit the top of the stool. Put
double-sided tape round
the side rim of the stool.
Stretch the cover over the
wadding and stick down,
keeping the stitching just
over the edge.

2 Stitch the braid
invisibly along the
top edge and then sew the
ends securely.

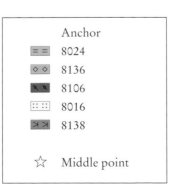

Anchor		
= =	8024	
◇ ◇	8136	
⊠ ⊠	8106	
⠇⠇	8016	
⊳ ⊳	8138	
☆	Middle point	

ALPHABET BLOCK

CELTIC
AND
MEDIEVAL

*Babies and toddlers will love this big, chunky brick.
It's easy to catch and so soft it won't hurt anyone.*

YOU WILL NEED

*18 x 109 cm (7 x 43 in) navy
14 count Aida, Zweigart E3246*

scissors

tacking (basting) thread

needle

embroidery hoop (frame)

*coton perlé no.5 DMC 554,
718, 725, 995, 996*

stranded cotton DMC 823

tapestry needle

spray starch

sewing thread

polyester stuffing

DMC	
══	554
⋮⋮	996
⊳⊳	725
◆◆	718
◥◥	995
Backstitch	
——	823
☆	Middle point

WORKING THE CROSS STITCH

Cut the Aida into 18 cm (7 in) squares and bind the edges to prevent fraying. Tack (baste) guidelines in the centre of each panel and work the cross stitch in coton perlé. Once complete, work the backstitch with two strands of stranded cotton. Press and spray starch onto the reverse side.

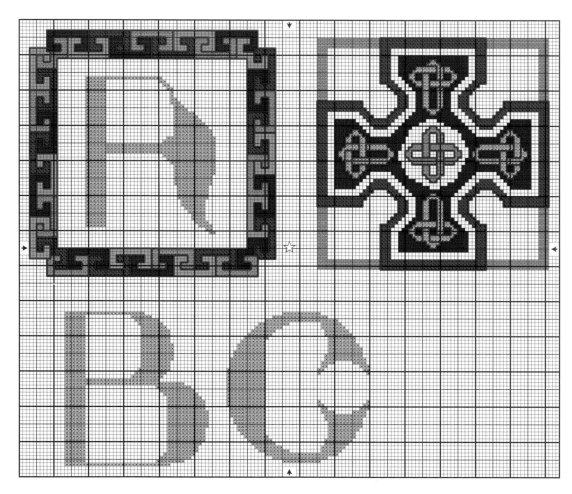

1 To make up: trim round each panel leaving four squares of Aida showing. Stitch the squares together as illustrated in the template section and turn the cube through to the right side. Ease out the corners and fill with stuffing.

2 Slip stitch the last two edges together and pat into shape.

GIFT TAG

Using the waste canvas technique, this handsome medieval bird could also be used to decorate a man's tie.

YOU WILL NEED

*15 cm (6 in) square of grey/blue
28 count Jobelan*

needle

*stranded cotton DMC 739,
740, 817, 3808*

tapestry needle

scissors

*small embroidery hoop
(flexihoop)*

tacking (basting) thread

stiff card (cardboard)

all-purpose glue

red gift tag

	DMC
🔲🔲	739
▶▶	740
══	3808
▪▪	817
	French knot
🌀	739
☆	Middle point

WORKING THE CROSS STITCH

Mark guidelines across the centre of the linen in both directions. Work the cross stitch over two threads using two strands of cotton. Once the cross stitch is complete, press on the wrong side before working the French knots.

1 To make up: measure the embroidered panel and cut a piece of stiff card (cardboard) the same size. Trim the fabric round the embroidery to 2 cm (¾ in) and stretch over the card, mitring the corners carefully. Stick the covered card onto the gift tag.

BOOKMARK

*Any book-lover would be delighted to receive this
beautiful, tasselled medieval bookmark which will bring a
distinguished academic air to any paperback.*

YOU WILL NEED

*8 x 20 cm (3 x 8 in) stitching
paper*

soft pencil

tapestry needle

*stranded cotton DMC 311, 312,
367, 918, 3046, 3722*

scissors

*5 cm (2 in) square of card
(cardboard)*

WORKING
THE CROSS STITCH

Mark the centre of the
stitching paper with a soft
pencil and work the cross
stitch design using three
strands of cotton.

NEEDLEWORK TIP

Be careful when using stitching paper since it tends
to rip easily if you have to unpick stitches. The
paper can be repaired if necessary with sticky tape
and the holes repunched using a sharp needle.

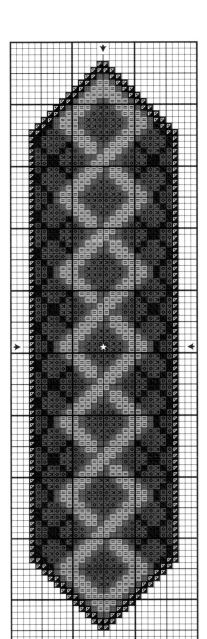

1 To make up: once
the design has been
completed trim away the
excess paper. Any paper
remaining visible can be
coloured using a felt pen.

2 Cut a 50 cm (20 in)
length of each
embroidery thread colour
and separate out the
strands. Wind the threads
round the card (cardboard)
and make a tassel to sew
onto one end of the
bookmark to complete.

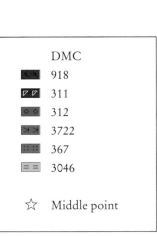

DMC

◾	918
▽▽	311
◇◇	312
➤➤	3722
⋮⋮	367
==	3046

☆ Middle point

SEWING KIT

Be prepared for any small repair jobs with this handy sewing kit which keeps everything you need together in one place.

YOU WILL NEED

18 x 38 cm (7 x 15 in) black 14 count Aida

embroidery hoop (frame)

tapestry needle

sewing thread

stranded cotton DMC 3 skeins 972, 1 skein each of 321, 796, 909, 995

scissors

28 x 69 cm (11 x 27 in) black iron-on interfacing

40 cm (16 in) square of black felt

5 x 13 cm (2 x 5 in) piece of wadding (batting)

5 x 13 cm (2 x 5 in) piece of stiff card (cardboard)

all-purpose glue

2 m (2¼ yd) of 25 mm (1 in) wide black bias binding

sewing machine

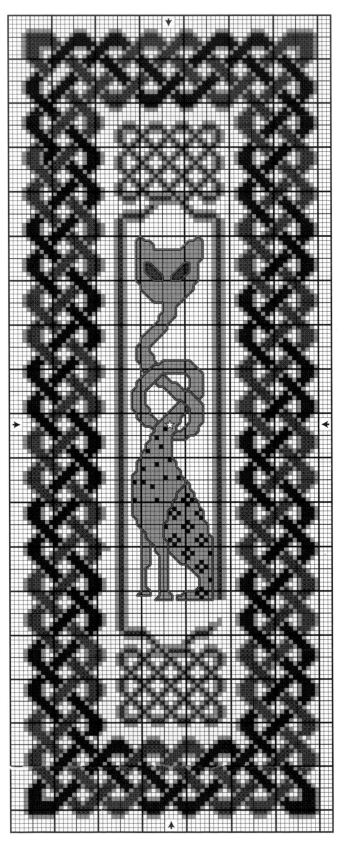

WORKING THE CROSS STITCH

Mark guidelines across the centre of the Aida in both directions and work the cross stitch using two strands of cotton. Work the backstitch with two strands of turquoise (995). Press on the reverse side.

DMC	
▬	321
▶	995
◤	796
⋮	972
◆	909

Backstitch

— 995

☆ Middle point

1 To make up: cut a piece of interfacing the same size as the Aida and iron onto the wrong side. Cut one piece of felt the same size, one 10 x 30 cm (4 x 12 in), another 10 x 18 cm (4 x 7 in) and the last piece 10 x 13 cm (4 x 5 in). Stick the wadding (batting) to the card (cardboard) and lay on top of the small piece of felt. Trim across the corners, stretch the felt and stick the flaps down.

2 Iron interfacing onto one side of the 10 x 30 cm (4 x 12 in) piece of felt for added strength and stitch in place on the backing felt. Pin the needle flap in position, lay the pin cushion pad along one edge and stitch securely.

3 Tack (baste) the completed felt backing onto the wrong side of the Aida. Stitch 3 mm (¼ in) all round, then remove the tacking (basting) thread. Fold a 76 cm (30 in) length of bias binding in half lengthways. Tuck in the ends and stitch close to the edge to make the ties. Fold the binding in half and tack in the middle of one end of the Aida. Pin and tack the rest of the bias binding round the edge of the sewing kit, mitring the corners neatly. Machine close to the edge of the binding to complete.

CELTIC KNOT SAMPLER

This unusual design features nine different Celtic knots.
You could stitch them individually to make a set of greetings cards.

YOU WILL NEED

25 cm (10 in) square of beige
28 count evenweave linen

tacking (basting) thread

needle

stranded cotton Anchor 187,
229

tapestry needle

embroidery hoop (frame)

20 cm (8 in) square of mount
board (backing board)

strong thread

picture frame

WORKING THE CROSS STITCH

Tack (baste) guidelines across the centre of the linen in both directions and work the cross stitch over two threads using two strands of cotton. Press the embroidery on the reverse side when complete.

1 To make up: stretch the piece of embroidery over the mount board (backing board).

2 Fit the sampler into a frame which complements the design.

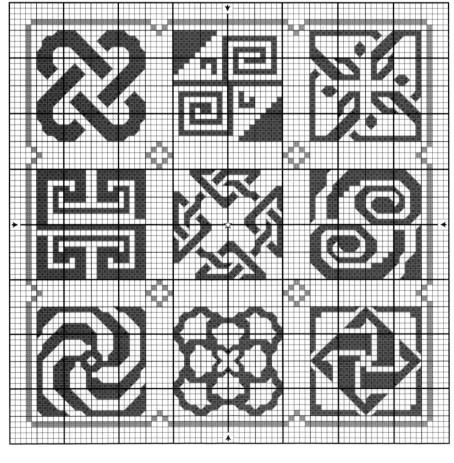

Anchor

▬ 229   ☆ Middle point

▦ 187

CELTIC CROSS

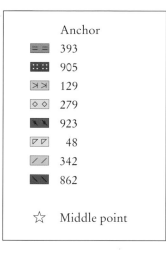

The Highlands of Scotland, with their wild landscapes and beautiful sunsets, are the backdrop for this quintessential Celtic cross.

	Anchor
== ==	393
∷∷∷	905
⋗ ⋗	129
◇ ◇	279
◣ ◥	923
▽ ▽	48
⁄ ⁄	342
▬ ▬	862
☆	Middle point

YOU WILL NEED

25 x 30 cm (10 x 12 in) pale blue 14 count Aida

tacking (basting) thread

needle

stranded cotton Anchor 48, 129, 279, 342, 393, 862, 923, 905

tapestry needle

embroidery hoop (frame)

18 x 23 cm (7 x 9 in) mount board (backing board)

strong thread

picture frame

WORKING THE CROSS STITCH

Tack (baste) guidelines across the centre of the Aida in both directions and work the cross stitch using two strands of cotton. Press the embroidery on the wrong side.

1 To make up: stretch the embroidery over the mount board (backing board).

2 Fit the design into a frame which complements it to complete.

BYZANTINE GIFT BAG

This little bag is the ideal size to hold a brooch or earrings.
The design was adapted from a Byzantine Gospel book.

YOU WILL NEED

40 cm (16 in) of 8 cm (3 in)
natural linen band,
Inglestone Collection 983/80

tacking (basting) thread

needle

stranded cotton Anchor 44,
306, 861

sewing thread

tapestry needle

pins

scissors

50 cm (20 in) ochre yellow cord

WORKING THE CROSS STITCH

Tack (baste) a guideline across the linen 15 cm (6 in) from one end and mark the centre line lengthways. This is the front of the bag and the motif faces towards the short end. Work the cross stitch and backstitch over two threads using two strands of thread. Once this is complete, press the embroidery on the wrong side and work the French knots as shown.

	Anchor		French knots
⊓⊓	306		
■	44	🌀	306
▦	861	◗	861
☆	Middle point		

1 To make up: fold over 5 cm (2 in) to the wrong side at both ends. Turn under 1 cm (3/8 in) and pin in place. Stitch across the hem close to the turned edge and again 1 cm (3/8 in) away to make a casing for the cord.

2 Fold the band in half crossways, with right side facing out. Stitch down both sides as far as the casing line.

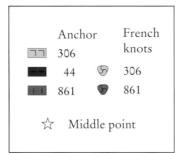

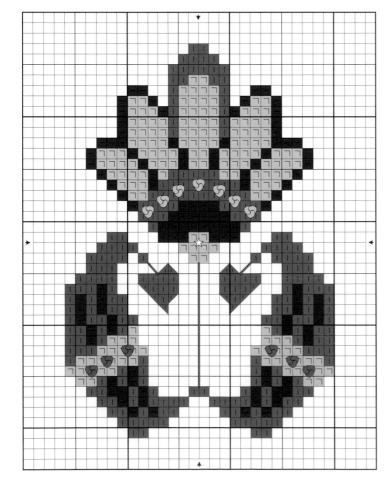

3 Cut the cord in two. Thread one piece through one way and then thread the other in the opposite direction. Tie the ends together with an overhand knot and unravel the ends to form simple tassels.

MEDIEVAL DOG PICTURE

This fascinating seventh century design has a dog whose tongue and tail have been elongated and interlaced to form an intricate pattern.

YOU WILL NEED

25 x 25 cm (10 x 10 in) cream 14 count Aida

stranded cotton Anchor 100, 310, 351, 859, 890

tapestry needle

interlocking bar frame

scissors

18 x 21 cm (7 x 8¼ in) mount board (backing board)

strong thread

picture frame

WORKING THE CROSS STITCH

Tack (baste) guidelines across the centre of the Aida in both directions and work the cross stitch and backstitch using two strands of thread. Press on the wrong side.

1 To make up: stretch the embroidery over the mount board (backing board) and fit in a suitable frame.

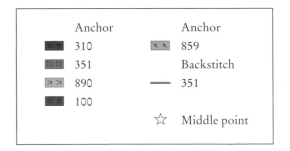

	Anchor		Anchor
▬▬	310	⋗⋗	859
⋮⋮⋮	351		Backstitch
⋗⋗	890	—	351
⊗⊗	100	☆	Middle point

LABYRINTH PAPERWEIGHT

This Celtic labyrinth design was inspired by a 300 BC coin from Knossos in Crete, home of the mythical Minotaur.

YOU WILL NEED

10 cm (4 in) square of 18 count single canvas

tacking (basting) thread

needle

coton perlé no.3 DMC 307, 796

tapestry needle

scissors

all-purpose glue

7 cm (2½ in) clear glass paperweight

8 cm (3 in) square of blue felt

◆ ◆ ◆ ◆ ◆

NEEDLEWORK TIP

The perlé thread is quite thick for this gauge of canvas, but it produces an attractive raised stitch.

WORKING THE CROSS STITCH

Tack (baste) guidelines across the centre of the canvas in both directions and work the cross stitch using a single strand of coton perlé.

1 To make up: trim the canvas to fit the bottom of the paperweight and stick in place around the outer edge. Cut the felt to size and glue over the canvas to complete.

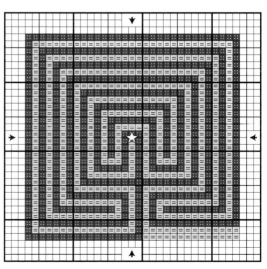

	DMC
= =	307
▓▓	796
☆	Middle point

BLACKWORK FRAME

Display a treasured old photograph in this tiny little frame. For a richer effect, work the embroidery over the whole of the frame area.

YOU WILL NEED

*30 x 60 cm (12 x 24 in) cream
27 count Linda, Zweigart
E1235*

scissors

needle

sewing thread

stranded cotton Anchor 403

fine gold braid Kreinik 002

tapestry needle

*20 cm (8 in) square of
mount board (backing board)*

craft knife

safety ruler

30 x 60 cm (12 x 24 in) calico

Anchor		Backstitch	
■	403	—	Anchor 403
☆	Middle point	=	Kreinik 002

WORKING THE CROSS STITCH

Cut a 15 x 30 cm (6 x 12 in) piece of linen. Tack (baste) guidelines across the centre in both directions. Work the cross stitch using two strands of cotton and the backstitch using one strand of black or gold thread. Press on the reverse side.

1 To make up: measure the outside edge of the embroidered panel and cut two pieces of mount board (backing board) that size. Measure the size of the centre panel and the distance from each edge. Use these measurements to cut a window in one piece of card (cardboard).

2 Trim the embroidered panel about 2½ cm (1 in) from the stitching. Cut into the corners of the window and stretch over the mount board frame. Stretch linen over the other piece of mount board.

3 Cut two pieces of calico 12 mm (½ in) larger than the frame and press over the turnings. Pin in place on the back of each part of the frame and hem. Oversew the two sections of the frame together along three sides.

4 Make a stand by scoring a piece of card 2½ cm (1 in) from the end and covering it in calico. Oversew the stand onto the back of the frame to complete.

EMBROIDERED BLOUSE

*These medieval motifs were inspired by the Book of Hours and will
match the waistcoat on the following page.*

YOU WILL NEED

white medieval-style blouse

scissors

14 count graph paper

pencil

double-sided tape

needle

tacking (basting) thread

tapestry needle

sewing thread

*stranded cotton Anchor white,
133, 246, 290, 335, 369, 380,
397, 398, 400, 403*

embroidery hoop (frame)

*30 cm (1/3 yd) black 27 count
Linda, Zweigart E1235*

pins

WORKING THE CROSS STITCH

Make the blouse using a similar
pattern or adapt a bought one to
suit the design. Trim the seam
allowance off the cuff and neck
facing pattern pieces. Lay the
pieces on 14 count graph paper
and draw an outline, then transfer
any pattern markings. Draw one
red flower in the centre of the cuff
and space both small flowers on
either side. Draw out the motifs
for the neck facing on separate
graph paper. Cut carefully round
the motifs and arrange them on
the pattern outline, keeping them
at least two squares from the edge,
and stick them in place.

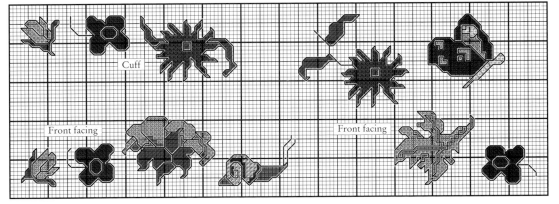

1 Draw an outline of
the pattern pieces on
the linen and tack (baste)
a central guideline. Work
the cross stitch and the
backstitch using two
strands of cotton over two
threads of linen.

2 To make up: once
complete, press on
the wrong side and cut out
adding 1½ cm (⅝ in) seam
allowances all round. Turn
under the seam allowance,
snipping the curves and
tack close to the edge.

3 Pin and tack onto the
blouse and slip stitch
in place. Make a small
loop from a bias strip to
fasten the cuffs and neck
opening and sew on the
buttons to complete the
fastenings.

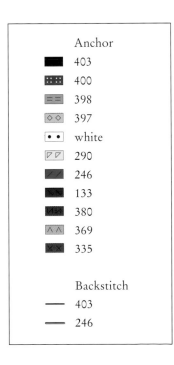

	Anchor
■	403
▓	400
= =	398
◇ ◇	397
• •	white
▽ ▽	290
▨	246
■	133
◧	380
∧ ∧	369
▨	335

	Backstitch
—	403
—	246

WAISTCOAT

This stunning design could also be added to an existing waistcoat using the waste canvas technique.

YOU WILL NEED

75 cm (⅞ yd) black 27 count Linda, Zweigart E1235

75 cm (⅞ yd) lining fabric

scissors

needle

sewing thread

sewing machine

14 count graph paper

pencil

double-sided tape

pins

tacking (basting) thread

stranded cotton Anchor 3 skeins each of white and 397, 2 skeins of 398 and one each of 133, 246, 290, 335, 369, 380, 400, 403

WORKING THE CROSS STITCH

Enlarge the pattern pieces or use a simple bought pattern and cut out the waistcoat front in linen. Sew the darts and press towards the centre. Trim the seam allowance from the pattern piece, then draw an outline on 14 count graph paper and transfer any pattern markings. Draw out the motifs on separate graph paper. Cut carefully round them and arrange on the pattern outline keeping them at least two squares from the edge. Once you are satisfied with the arrangement, stick them in place. Mark the outline of the unicorn and work the cross stitch from the chart. Sew the backstitch to finish the embroidery. Work the other side of the waistcoat as a mirror image of the first side and press both front panels on the reverse side.

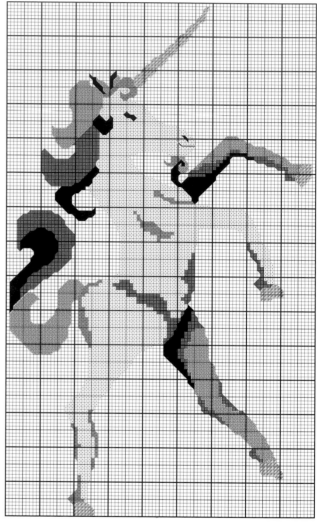

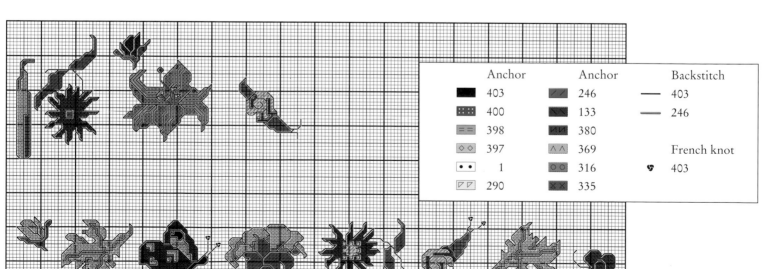

Anchor		Anchor		Backstitch	
■	403	⁄⁄	246	—	403
▦	400	＼＼	133	—	246
＝＝	398	ИИ	380		
◇◇	397	＾＾	369	French knot	
••	1	○○	316	❥	403
▽▽	290	✕✕	335		

1 To make up: cut out the front lining and two backs in lining fabric. Sew all the darts and press. With right sides together, stitch the front lining to the linen leaving the shoulder and side seams free. Stitch the back pieces together along the armhole edge, the neck edge and the bottom. Trim the seam allowances and snip across the corners before turning through.

Pin and sew the back and front together at the shoulder and side seams, leaving the lining free. Trim the seams and press flat.

2 Turn under the lining seam allowance and slip stitch. Press the waistcoat on the reverse side and add a fastening if required.

MONASTIC BELL PULL

*The beads on this beautiful design catch the light
and give it a special richness.*

YOU WILL NEED

*25 x 92 cm (10 x 36 in) navy
14 count Aida, Zweigart E3706*

rotating frame

needle

tacking (basting) thread

scissors

tapestry needle

*Anchor Marlitt 3 skeins of 817,
1007 and 5 skeins of 859*

*two packets of glass seed beads,
Mill Hill shade 02009*

*fine metallic braid Kreinik 012,
026*

*silver thread Madeira no.5 9805
shade 10*

sewing thread

sewing machine

tailor's chalk

*two packets of frosted glass
beads, Mill Hill shade 62034*

pins

*25 x 92 cm (10 x 36 in)
navy cotton backing fabric*

*8¹⁄₂ x 13¹⁄₂ cm (3¹⁄₄ x 5¹⁄₄ in)
card (cardboard)*

30 cm (12 in) silver cord

WORKING THE CROSS STITCH

Tack (baste) a guideline lengthways down the centre of the Aida. Begin stitching about 13 cm (5 in) from the top using two strands of Marlitt. Work all the cross stitch and then the Smyrna cross stitch. Once these are complete, sew on the beads and finally work the backstitch. Remove the embroidery from the rotating frame and block if necessary.

Anchor Marlitt	
▦	1007
⠿	817
▶▶	859
Madiera metallic silver	
—	9805
Kreinik metallic	
◇◇	balger fine braid 026
◥◥	balger fine braid 012
Mill Hill beads	
▽▽	62034
◿◿	02009

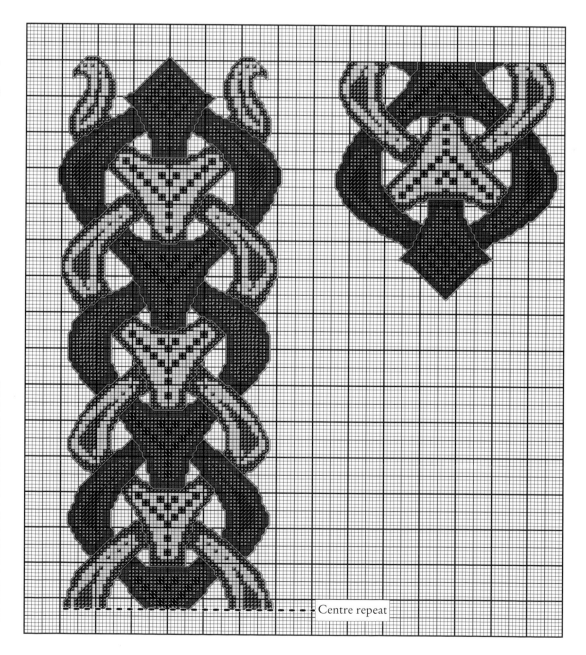

Centre repeat

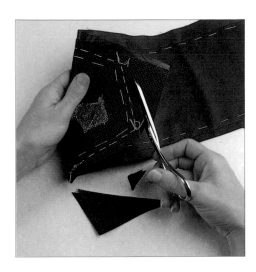

1 To make up: tack a guideline down both sides of the embroidery about 1½ cm (½ in) from the stitching. Mark the point of the bell pull 3½ cm (1½ in) down from the stitching and draw a diagonal line from this mark to the side guidelines. Complete the tacking (basting) and pin to the cotton backing with the right sides together. Stitch round the bell pull along the guideline leaving it open at the top. Trim the seams and cut across the corners before turning through.

2 Ease out the corners and press on the reverse side. Turn over a 6 cm (2½ in) hem and stitch securely by hand. Score the card (cardboard) in the middle lengthways and insert into the hem. Thread the cord through, tie the ends together and tuck inside the hem. Make a tassel and stitch it to the point of the bell pull to finish off.

TRINKET BOWL

This pretty frosted glass bowl is decorated with a Celtic motif adapted
from a design on an ornate Saxon dagger.

YOU WILL NEED

15 cm (6 in) square of antique
white 28 count Cashel linen,
Zweigart E3281

tacking (basting) thread

needle

tapestry needle

small embroidery frame
(flexihoop)

stranded cotton DMC 926, 3808

fine antique gold braid
Kreinik 221

9 cm (3½ in) frosted glass bowl,
Framecraft GT4

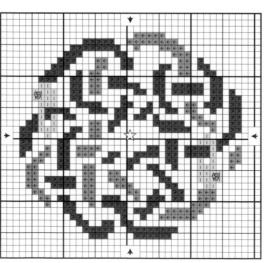

	Kreinik fine braid
I I	Antique gold 221
	DMC
↗↗	3808
←←	926
	French knot
●	926
☆	Middle point

WORKING THE CROSS STITCH

Tack (baste) guidelines across the
centre of the linen in both directions.
Work the cross stitch using two
strands of cotton and a single strand
of gold thread. Press on the reverse
side and then work the French knots
to complete the design.

1 To make up: fit the piece of
embroidery into the lid of the glass
bowl following the manufacturer's
instructions.

GREETINGS CARD

The Book of Kells is a rich source of inspiration for medieval embroidery and these two loving doves are just one example.

YOU WILL NEED

*15 cm (6 in) square of cream
28 count evenweave linen*

tacking (basting) thread

needle

*small embroidery hoop
(flexihoop)*

tapestry needle

*stranded cotton DMC 367,
3046, 3722*

scissors

*7 cm (2¾ in) square of cream
felt*

*greetings card with
a 6½ cm (2½ in) opening*

double-sided tape

✦✦✦✦✦

NEEDLECRAFT TIP

Use double-sided tape
to mount the
embroidered panel to
prevent the card from
buckling.

WORKING THE CROSS STITCH

Tack (baste) guidelines across the centre in both directions. Work the cross stitch using one strand of cotton over single threads of linen.

1 To make up: press on the reverse side once complete and trim to fit inside the card. Trim the felt to the size of the opening and stick on the inside flap. Use double-sided tape to stick the embroidery behind the opening and stick the flap down firmly.

DMC	
▬▬	3722
⣀⣀	3046
➤➤	367
☆	Middle point

MEDIEVAL CLOCK

This clock design was inspired by the magnificent architecture and bright colourful stained glass windows found in medieval churches.

YOU WILL NEED

25 x 30 cm (10 x 12 in) black 14 count Aida

tacking (basting) thread

needle

tapestry needle

interlocking bar frame

2 reels of fine Aztec gold braid Kreinik 202HL

stranded cotton DMC 340, 347, 351, 444, 445, 988, 995, 996, 3348, 3746

25 x 30 cm (10 x 12 in) lightweight iron-on interfacing

MDF (medium density fibreboard) clock base and mechanism, Decorative Arts W122

blackboard paint

paintbrush

scissors

pins

tailor's chalk

all-purpose glue

WORKING THE CROSS STITCH

Tack (baste) guidelines across the centre of the Aida in both directions. Work the cross stitch using two strands of cotton and one strand of gold braid. The central stitch on the chart is shown for reference only to ensure accurate placement of the clock mechanism at the end of the project. Once complete, press on the reverse side and iron on the interfacing.

1 To make up: paint the MDF clock base with two coats of blackboard paint and leave to dry.

2 Make a pattern by pressing a piece of A4 paper over the clock base. Cut around the marked line and cut out the centre hole. Lay the pattern on the embroidery. Once you have checked it is central and square, pin in place and cut out carefully.

3 Spread glue over the MDF base and stick down the embroidered panel. Make a cord using a reel of fine braid. Stick this round the rim, trim the ends and tuck underneath the Aida. Snip away the fabric covering the hole and fit the clock mechanism following the manufacturer's instructions.

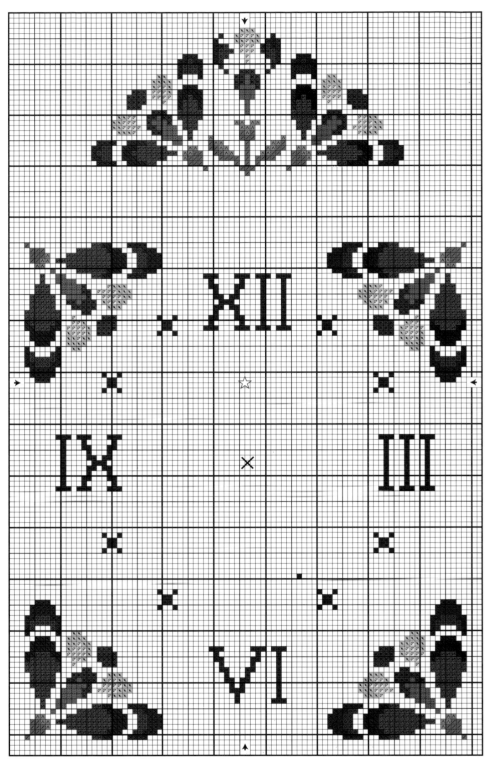

DMC		
⋯ 340		ИИ 996
347		∧∧ 3348
◇◇ 351		⋈⋈ 3746
444		Kreinik fine
▽▽ 445		braid 202HL
∕∕ 988		☆ Middle point
995		

WOOL SCARF

This motif comes from the border design of a splendid illuminated manuscript from the renowned Winchester school of the early eleventh century.

YOU WILL NEED

dark green wool scarf

*10 cm (4 in) square
of 14 count waste canvas*

tacking (basting) thread

scissors

embroidery needle

*stranded cotton Anchor 891,
901*

fine gold braid Kreinik 002

sewing thread

*10 cm (4 in) square of
dark green felt*

	Anchor
4 4	901
▽ ▽	891
	Kreinik fine
—	gold braid 002
☆	Middle point

WORKING THE CROSS STITCH

Tack (baste) the waste canvas centrally at one end of the scarf about 5 cm (2 in) up from the fringe. Work the cross stitch using two strands of cotton. Take care to sew the stitches as evenly as possible, bringing the needle up exactly where the last stitch finished.

1 To make up: once complete, remove the waste canvas thread by thread. This will be easier if you manipulate the canvas first to loosen the threads. Work the backstitch using a single strand of gold braid.

2 Press the embroidery on the reverse side once complete. Cut a circle from the dark green felt to cover the back of the embroidery and then sew invisibly to the scarf.

SPIRAL TRAY CLOTH

This early medieval design is typical of those from Iona, Scotland, and illustrated in The Book of Durrow.

YOU WILL NEED

25 x 40 cm (10 x 16 in) sage 27 count evenweave linen

tacking (basting) thread

needle

tapestry needle

embroidery hoop (frame)

stranded cotton Anchor 118, 300, 307, 969

scissors

sewing thread

WORKING THE CROSS STITCH

Tack (baste) guidelines across the centre of the linen in both directions. Work the cross stitch and backstitch using two strands of cotton over two threads.

1 To make up: when complete, press the embroidery on the wrong side. Turn under a 12 mm (1/2 in) hem on all edges, mitring the corners and stitch in place by hand or sewing machine.

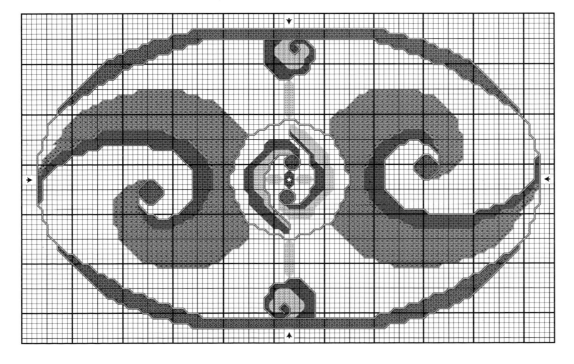

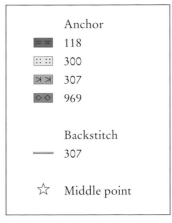

Anchor

▨	118
⋮⋮	300
⧂	307
◈	969

Backstitch

— 307

☆ Middle point

SPECTACLE CASE

*Your spectacles will never be lost again
if kept in this attractive case which can be hung around your neck.*

WORKING THE CROSS STITCH

Tack (baste) guidelines across the centre of the canvas in both directions. Work the perlé cross stitch on the birds first, then use the coton à broder to fill in. Finally work the background. Press the embroidery on the wrong side and trim the canvas to 1 cm (½ in). Snip into curves, turn the edges in and tack.

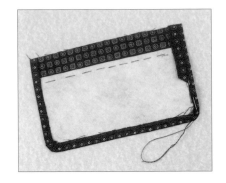

1 To make up: cut two pieces of interfacing 8.3 x 17.2 cm (3¼ x 6¾ in) and round off the corners. Iron these onto the silk and cut out leaving a 1 cm (½ in) seam allowance. Turn the edges over and tack carefully, easing in the fullness at the corners.

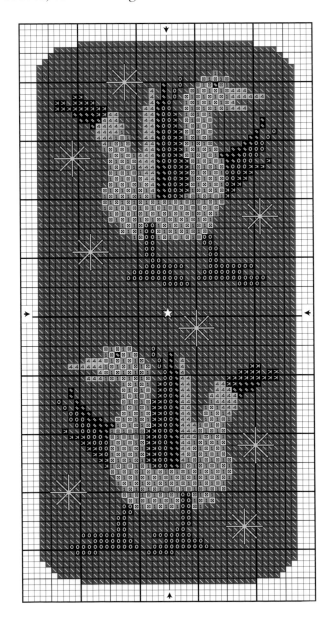

2 Put the canvas and lining pieces together with right sides facing out and oversew the edges. Once both are stitched round, put the spectacle case together and oversew with coton perlé 930, starting and finishing 5 cm (2 in) down from the top edge.

DMC	
◣◣	310
1 1	783
4 4	972
◥◥	796
◥◥	930
○○	321
⊠⊠	coton à broder 745

Backstitch
— DMC Art.284

☆ Middle point

3 Tie a knot in the cord 4 cm (1½ in) from the end and tease out the end. Take the frayed ends over the knot and tie tightly, then pull the ends back down over the knot and wrap thread round them to make a waist for the tassel. Repeat at the other end, trim the ends neatly and stitch to each side of the spectacle case as shown.

RINGBEARER'S CUSHION

This delightful Celtic design could be stitched in two complementary colours to match the bridesmaids' dresses or the wedding flowers.

YOU WILL NEED

30 cm (12 in) square of antique white 28 count linen

tacking (basting) thread

needle

stranded cotton DMC 224, 3685

tapestry needle

embroidery hoop (frame)

1 m (1¼ yd) of 2 cm (¾ in) wine coloured ribbon

1 m (1¼ yd) piping cord

sewing thread

sewing machine

scissors

30 cm (12 in) square of antique white backing fabric

polyester stuffing

1 m (1¼ yd) 3 mm (¼ in) wine coloured ribbon

WORKING THE CROSS STITCH

Tack (baste) guidelines across the centre of the linen in both directions. Work the centre motif using two strands of cotton. Count out the threads carefully and stitch the border. Press on the reverse side.

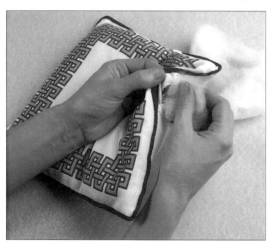

1 To make up: fold the wide ribbon over the piping cord and tack in position round the edge of the cushion 2 cm (¾ in) away from the cross stitch. Stitch the piping in place along one side. With right sides facing, sew the cushion cover together along the remaining three sides. Trim across the corners and turn through. Give the cushion a final press and fill with stuffing.

2 Slip stitch the opening. Cut the narrow ribbon in half, find the middle of each half and sew securely in the centre of the cross. Stitch a decorative cross stitch on top to finish.

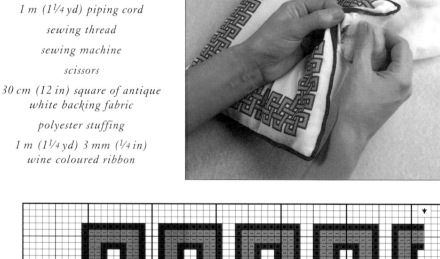

DMC	
– –	224
● ● ●	3685
☆	Middle point

CHESSBOARD

The black squares are stitched in Assisi embroidery,
a variation of cross stitch where the design areas are left blank and the
background is filled with cross stitch.

YOU WILL NEED

38 cm (15 in) square of white
14 count Aida

tacking (basting) thread

needle

scissors

embroidery hoop (frame)

stranded cotton Anchor 403

tapestry needle

safety ruler

30 x 60 cm (12 x 24 in)
mount board (backing board)

craft knife

strong thread

all-purpose glue

125 cm (1⅓ yd) black cord

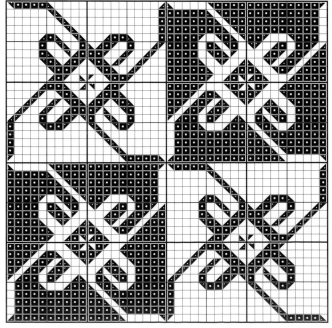

WORKING THE CROSS STITCH

Tack (baste) guidelines across the centre of the Aida in both directions and work the cross stitch using two strands of cotton. Press the embroidery on the wrong side.

1 To make up: measure the length of two adjacent sides of the embroidery. Cut two pieces of mount board (backing board) that size and stretch the embroidery over one of them.

2 Oversew the cord to the edge of the chessboard. Unravel the ends and stitch them flat underneath the board. Stick the second piece of mount board (backing board) to the bottom of the chessboard to cover the raw edges.

Anchor
■■ 403

56

BEDSIDE TABLECLOTH

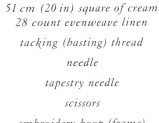

This unusual Celtic design could be repeated on the border of a much larger tablecloth.

YOU WILL NEED

51 cm (20 in) square of cream 28 count evenweave linen

tacking (basting) thread

needle

tapestry needle

scissors

embroidery hoop (frame)

Anchor Marlitt 831, 1140

gold thread DMC Art.284

sewing thread

	Anchor Marlitt
⬛••	831
⬛	1140
	Backstitch
—	DMC Art.284
☆	Middle point

WORKING THE CROSS STITCH

Tack (baste) guidelines across the centre of the linen in both directions. Count the threads out to the border on all four guidelines and double-check the spacing before beginning to sew.

1 To make up: first, sew the cross stitch onto the centre motif using a single strand of Marlitt thread over two threads of linen, then work the backstitch in gold thread. Once the design is complete, press the embroidery on the wrong side.

2 Trim away the excess fabric, leaving 2½ cm (1 in) all round for the hem i.e. a 46 cm (18 in) square. Mitre the corners and make a 12 mm (½ in) hem all round. Tack in position, then hem. Slip stitch the mitred corners and press on the wrong side to finish.

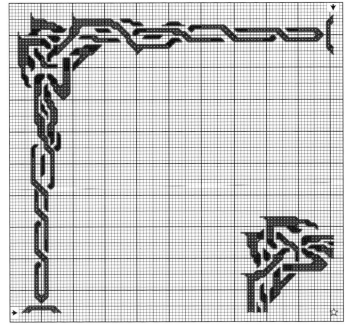

PURSE

This handy little purse with a bold dragon design could be used for holding game counters, money or a spare lipstick.

YOU WILL NEED

18 x 36 cm (7 x 14 in) black 14 count Aida

scissors

tacking (basting) thread

needle

interlocking bar frame

tapestry needle

stranded cotton DMC white, 742, 744, 900, 910

fine Aztec gold braid Kreinik 202HL

18 x 36 cm (7 x 14 in) medium weight iron-on interfacing

18 x 36 cm (7 x 14 in) black lining

sewing thread

sewing machine

8 cm (3 in) black zip

WORKING THE CROSS STITCH

Cut an 18 cm (7 in) square of Aida and tack (baste) guidelines across the centre in both directions. Work the cross stitch using two strands of cotton and finish with the backstitch. Once complete, press the reverse side of the embroidery and iron the interfacing onto both pieces of Aida.

1 To make up: draw out a template and use it to cut out two purse shapes from the lining and the Aida, making sure that the cross stitch is positioned within the stitching line. With right sides together, sew the lining to the Aida along the straight edge. Trim the seams and press open. Pin the two sections together, matching the seams, and stitch round, leaving a 5 cm (2 in) gap in the lining.

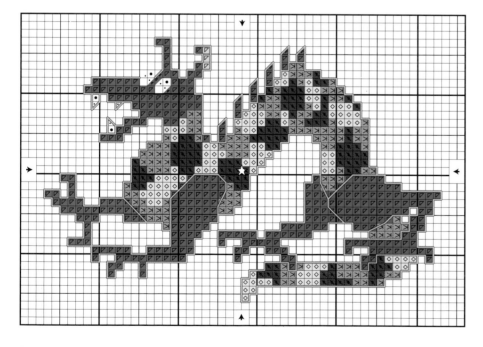

2 Trim the seam allowance and snip the curves before turning through. Slipstitch the lining and tuck it inside the purse. Sew the zip in the opening by hand, using a double length of thread.

DMC			Backstitch
• •	1	■ 900	— Kreinik fine braid 202HL
▶▶	742	◢ 910	
◇◇	744		☆ Middle point

BOOK COVER

Inspired by a medieval stone carving this bird design could
be used to cover a small notebook or sketchbook.

YOU WILL NEED

25 x 38 cm (10 x 15 in) cream
14 count Aida

tacking (basting) thread

needle

embroidery hoop (frame)

tapestry needle

stranded cotton Anchor 371,
942, 943

scissors

25 x 38 cm (10 x 15 in) medium
weight iron-on interfacing

small notebook, approximate
size 11 x 15½ cm (4⅜ x 6 in)

pins

double-sided tape

WORKING THE CROSS STITCH

Tack (baste) a guideline crossways down the middle of the Aida to mark the position of the book spine. Tack another line 6 cm (2⅜ in) away marking the centre of the design. Find the mid-point of this line and mark with tacking (basting) thread. Begin the cross stitch, making sure that the bird is upright on the right hand side of the Aida. Once the embroidery is complete, remove the tacking (basting) thread and press.

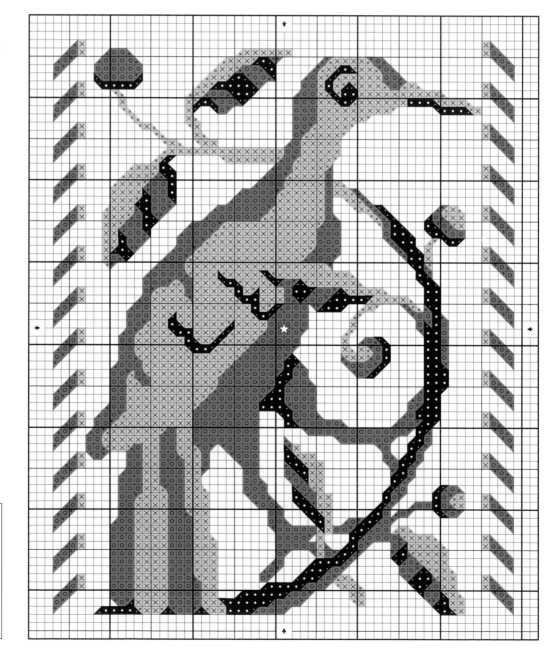

Anchor
✕✕ 942
⊙⊙ 943
∴∴ 371
☆ Middle point

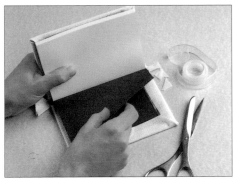

1 To make up: iron the interfacing on the reverse side and mark the position of the book spine with pins.

2 Lay the fabric face down and hold the book in line with the pins. Open the front flap of the book and trim the fabric to 2½ cm (1 in) all round. Cut across the corners 1 cm (³/8 in) from the book and snip into the spine.

3 Stick double-sided tape round the inside of the cover. First fold over the corners, then stretch the cover onto the tape. Repeat on the other side, making sure that the book can close easily. Tuck the spare Aida down inside the spine with the point of small scissors. Use more double-sided tape to stick the fly leaf down on both sides.

BLACKWORK DECORATIONS

Although traditionally black on white or cream fabric, these "Blackwork" Christmas decorations look equally good worked in red on black fabric.

YOU WILL NEED

pencil

craft knife

thin card (cardboard)

scissors

15 x 30 cm (6 x 12 in) cream or black 27 count Linda, Zweigart E1235

vanishing marker pen

flexihoop (small embroidery frame)

tapestry needle

stranded cotton Anchor 47, 275, 403

fine gold braid Kreinik 002

needle

sewing thread

WORKING THE CROSS STITCH

Trace the template and cut out three card (card-board) shapes for each decoration. Place the shape on the linen and draw three outlines using the vanishing marker pen. Stitch the blackwork design inside the lines and press on the wrong side.

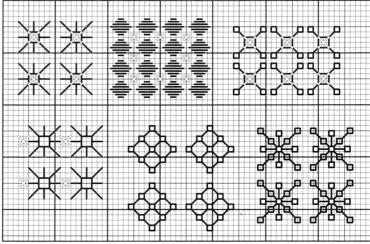

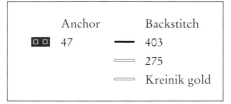

	Anchor		Backstitch
▣▢	47	——	403
		═	275
		══	Kreinik gold

	Anchor	
	——	403
	═	Kreinik gold

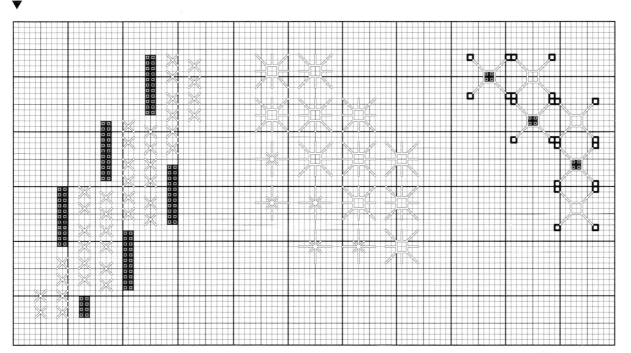

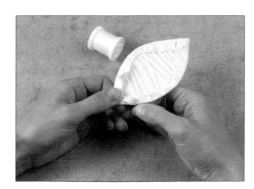

1 To make up: stretch the pieces of linen over each of the card shapes using a double length of sewing thread.

2 Make a 10 cm (4 in) loop of gold braid and sew it to the top of one panel on the wrong side. Hold two of the shapes together and oversew the edges together. Stitch the third panel in place to make a three-dimensional decoration.

3 Cut a 5 cm (2 in) square of card. Mix some black and gold thread and wrap them round the card several times. Tie a loop of gold at the top and cut the threads at the bottom. Wrap a length of gold thread round the tassel to make the waist and tie off. Trim the ends and sew onto the bottom of the decoration.

TEMPLATES

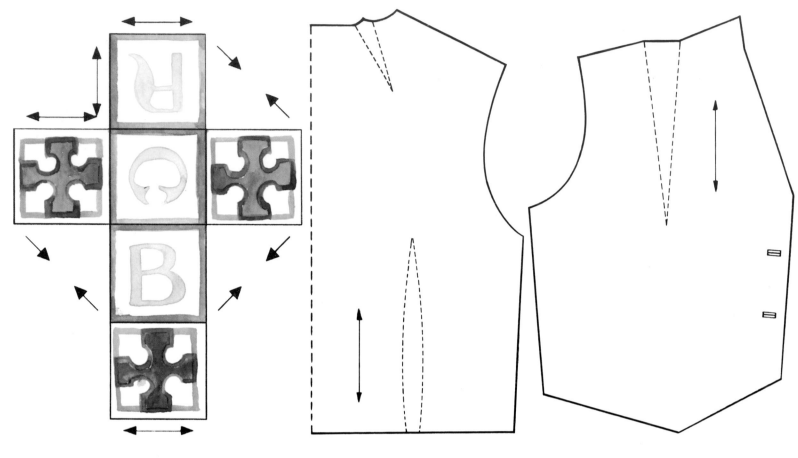

ALPHABET BLOCK

WAISTCOAT

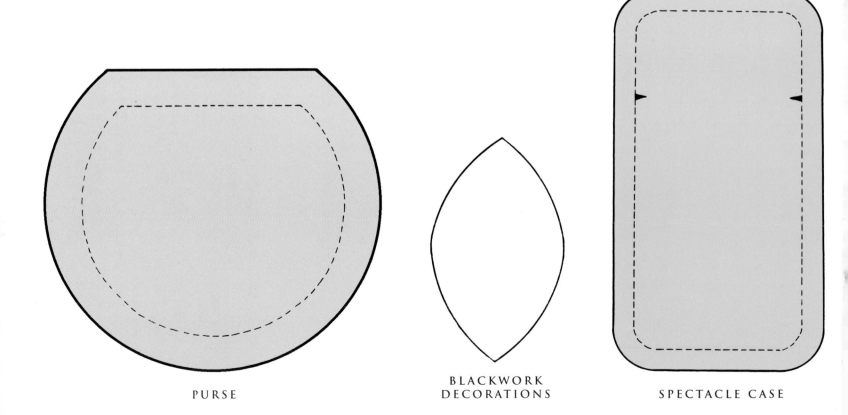

PURSE

BLACKWORK
DECORATIONS

SPECTACLE CASE